01-15

WORLD RELIGIONS
JUDAISM

BY NATALIE M. ROSINSKY

Content Adviser:
Michael L. Satlow, Ph.D.,
Program in Judaic Studies,
Department of Religious Studies, Brown University

Reading Adviser:
Alexa L. Sandmann, Ed.D., Professor of Literacy,
College and Graduate School of Education,
Health, and Human Services, Kent State University

Compass Point Books
151 Good Counsel Drive
P.O. Box 669
Mankato, MN 56002-0669

 This book was manufactured with paper containing
at least 10 percent post-consumer waste.

Photographs ©: Alamy: ecomedia/Robert B. Fishman 38, Miriam Reik 26;
AP Photo: John Baer 36–37; Art Resource, N.Y.: Bildarchiv Preussischer
Kulturbesitz 34; Corbis: Bettmann 17, Lebrecht Music & Arts 32, Saba/J.A.
Giordano 9; Getty Images: AFP 39, AFP/Menahem Kahana 40–41, AFP/
Patrick Baz 6, GPO/Zoltan Kluger 35, Kitra Cahana 4–5, Mark Wilson 42,
Time Life Pictures/Mansell 10–11; The Granger Collection, New York 28–29;
iStockphoto: Barbara Sauder 20–21, Mike Cherim 23, Mikhail Levit cover, Tova
Teitelbaum 24; North Wind Picture Archives 16; Shutterstock: Aron Brand
(design element) cover (middle and bottom), back cover (left) and throughout,
Dejan Gileski 15, maga (background texture) 4, 10, 20, 28, 36, 46, 47, Marek
Slusarczyk (Star of David design element) cover (top and bottom), back cover
(top), 1, 45, sidebars throughout, Mikhail Levit 18.

Editor: Brenda Haugen
Designers: Ashlee Suker and Bobbie Nuytten
Media Researcher: Svetlana Zhurkin
Library Consultant: Kathleen Baxter
Art Director: LuAnn Ascheman-Adams
Creative Director: Joe Ewest
Editorial Director: Nick Healy
Managing Editor: Catherine Neitge
Cartographer: XNR Productions, Inc.

Library of Congress Cataloging-in-Publication Data
Rosinsky, Natalie M. (Natalie Myra)
  Judaism / by Natalie M. Rosinsky.
    p. cm.—(World religions)
  Includes index.
  ISBN 978-0-7565-4240-5 (library binding)
  1. Judaism—Juvenile literature. I. Title. II. Series.
  BM573.R67 2009
  296—dc22   2009015813

Visit Compass Point Books on the Internet at *www.compasspointbooks.com*
or e-mail your request to *custserv@compasspointbooks.com*

Table of Contents

Chapter One

FLIGHTS TO FREEDOM

The thin, barefoot people cheered as they stepped off an airplane in Israel. Some bent down to kiss the ground. For these Ethiopian Jews, this May morning in 1991 was the most important day of their lives.

They had overcome many hardships to reach this Promised Land of their religion, Judaism.

Israel's Operation Solomon used 34 large airplanes to rescue more than 14,000 Jews in Ethiopia from starvation and political oppression. The hostile Ethiopian government had given pilots just 36 hours to complete this rescue. One cargo plane carried more than twice the usual number of passengers—a record-breaking 1,087 people. Seats were removed to squeeze them all in. Other planes were so packed that two or three weary, hungry people were squeezed into each seat. Some planes even added passengers during flight—five babies were born between the planes' takeoffs and landings. Their mothers had chosen to make this important journey despite their pregnancies.

Their story is remarkable because these Jews had lived simple lives, far from modern technology. Most had never even seen an airplane. Sirak M. Sabahat was 9 years old when he was a passenger on one of the planes. He said his people thought the plane was a big bird. Sabahat, who was born in Ethiopia, describes his experience as stepping from the 19th century straight into the 20th century. A reporter who flew

An Ethiopian woman clutched Israeli flags after a four-hour flight from Ethiopia to Israel.

 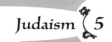

Ethiopian Jews crowded into a plane to make the trip from Ethiopia to Israel in 1991.

to Israel with these frightened, excited immigrants declared upon their arrival: "They're ending a trip of 3,000 years."

The religious devotion of the Ethiopian Jews, who call themselves the Beta Israel (House of Israel), had lasted more than 3,000 years. They believe their worship goes back to the time of King Solomon of ancient Israel. They believe he was their ancestor. Isolated from

Jewish Demographics

More than 13 million Jews live around the globe. That is less than 1 percent of the world's population. More than 5 million Jews live in the United States, and about another 5 million live in Israel. France, Canada, the United Kingdom, Russia, and Argentina have Jewish populations ranging between 180,000 and 500,000 people. The rest of the Jewish world population is scattered across the globe in nearly 100 other countries.

much of the world until 1860, the Beta Israel practice ancient Jewish customs. For hundreds of years, they believed they were the only Jews left alive. Yet the Beta Israel refused to convert to other religions. They remained faithful to Judaism. They endured the prejudice and oppression of many of their neighbors, who scornfully called Ethiopian Jews *falashas*, which means "outsiders."

Operation Solomon reunited many Beta Israel families in the Holy Land, since about 8,800 other Ethiopian Jews had been airlifted to Israel in 1984 and 1985. The

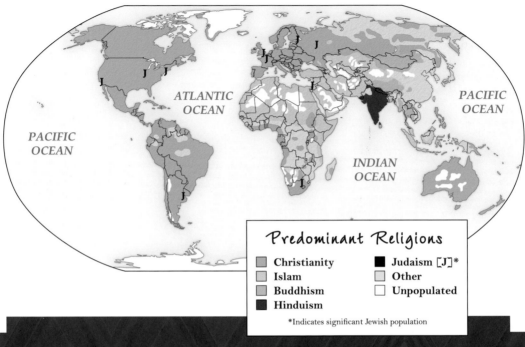

Predominant Religions

- Christianity
- Islam
- Buddhism
- Hinduism
- Judaism [J]*
- Other
- Unpopulated

*Indicates significant Jewish population

Jewish Identity

Who is a Jew? Jewish law declares that birth rather than belief makes someone Jewish. Anyone born to a Jewish mother is considered by Jewish law to be a Jew. Some Jewish leaders also consider the children of Jewish fathers to be Jews as long as they participate in an act of Jewish identity, such as circumcision or immersion. Someone may convert from another religion to Judaism by studying it with a rabbi, a Jewish religious leader, but this isn't strictly required. However, most rabbis require the rituals of circumcision and immersion for conversion.

Jews who do not worship in traditional ways or even believe in God are still classified as Jews by Jewish laws. These Jews may still feel strong ties to Jewish history and customs.

A young Ethiopian Jew gazed through the fence at the Israeli Embassy in Addis Ababa, Ethiopia, while waiting to receive documents to emigrate.

earlier rescue missions were called Operation Moses and Operation Joshua. At those times, the Beta Israel walked for months to reach the airfield in Sudan, but only about a third of them were permitted to leave the country.

The experiences of the Beta Israel and their devotion to Israel are part of the history of Judaism.

Chapter Two
FOUNDERS AND BELIEFS

Judaism is one of the world's oldest monotheistic religions—faiths whose followers worship just one God. It began at a time and in a place where people worshipped many gods. The ancient inhabitants of the Fertile Crescent—a half-moon-shaped area of land that today is mainly in Israel, Jordan, Syria, and Iraq—believed that many gods controlled events. A sky god, they thought, created rain, while an earth god was responsible for crops. Other gods, they said, determined health, luck, and success in war or hunting.

These peoples made statues to represent their gods and placed them in temples. Some inhabitants of this area were city dwellers, part of large civilizations. Others, like the tribe said to be led by Abraham, who later became the founder of Judaism, belonged to smaller groups that had no homeland and wandered from place to place.

According to the Torah, God spoke to Abraham around 2000 B.C.E. The Torah says God told Abraham that if he led his people to another land and worshipped only God,

To acknowledge all world religions, Compass Point Books uses new abbreviations to distinguish time periods. For ancient times, instead of B.C., we use B.C.E., which means before the common era. B.C. means before Christ. Similarly we use C.E., which means in the common era, instead of A.D. The abbreviation A.D. stands for the Latin phrase anno Domini, which means in the year of our Lord, referring to Jesus Christ. Of course not all peoples worship Jesus.

According to the Torah, Abraham offered his son Isaac as a sacrifice to God.

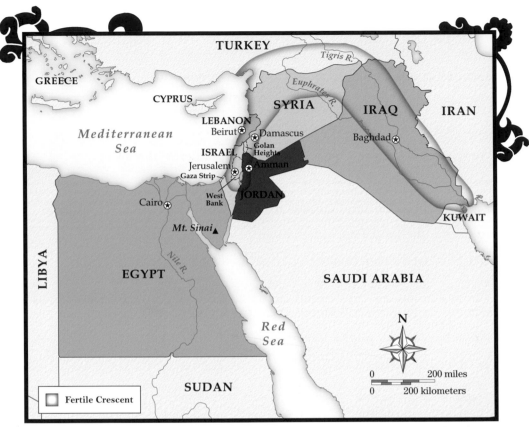

The Fertile Crescent included several of the countries in what is now called the Middle East. The area once known as Canaan today roughly fits into the areas occupied by Israel and Lebanon.

Abraham's descendants would one day become a great nation. Abraham entered into this covenant (agreement) with God. He led his band of nomads on a journey toward what was then the land of Canaan.

Even though Abraham was 100 years old and his wife, Sarah, was 75 years old, God granted their wish for a son, the Torah says. Sarah gave birth to Isaac. Later God tested Abraham's loyalty by asking him to kill Isaac.

Abraham agreed, but at the last minute God spared Isaac. Again God promised Abraham that his family would grow into a great nation. Followers of the world religions of Christianity, Islam, and the Baha'i faith also consider Abraham one of their religious patriarchs (leaders).

According to the Torah, Isaac's son Jacob had 12 sons, who founded the 12 tribes of Israel (Israel is another name for Jacob). Their descendants, known as Israelites, were later enslaved by the ruler of Egypt, its pharoah. After years of suffering, they escaped slavery with the help of God. Their leader, Moses, received permission from the pharaoh to lead the Jews out of Egypt after God sent 10 frightening plagues. According

Passover

During the springtime holiday of Passover, Jews remember and celebrate their ancestors' escape to freedom. At a special family meal called a seder, they tell the story of fleeing Egypt. They eat special foods that represent the bitterness of slavery, the bricks they used as slaves, and the hurried nature of their escape. Jews eat unleavened bread called *matzoh* during Passover because their ancestors didn't have time while fleeing to let their bread dough rise. This holiday is called Passover because God caused the most terrible plague sent to Egypt—one that killed first-born sons—to skip or "pass over" Jewish homes.

to the Torah, this journey, called the Exodus, took place around 1250 B.C.E. Despite giving permission for the Israelites to leave, the pharoah had no intention of keeping his word. He sent his army to stop the Israelites. During the Exodus, God is said to have parted the Red Sea to help the Israelites escape the pharoah's army.

During the 40 years that Moses led the Jews, the Torah says, he received God's teachings on Mount Sinai. He came down from the mountaintop carrying stone tablets miraculously engraved with the Ten Commandments.

The Ten Commandments

1. Worship no other gods.
2. Do not worship idols.
3. Do not misuse the name of the Lord.
4. Keep the Sabbath holy.
5. Honor your father and mother.
6. Do not murder.
7. Do not commit adultery.
8. Do not steal.
9. Do not give false testimony.
10. Do not covet.

Symbols of Judaism

A seven-branched candleholder called a menorah became a symbol of Judaism. It's said that on Mount Sinai God told Moses to create a menorah.

A menorah sculpture in Jerusalem

The Shield of David, also called the Star of David, is another symbol of Judaism. This ancient symbol was first widely used by Jews in 14th century Czechoslovakia. Today this six-pointed star appears on the blue and white flag of Israel.

These tablets have come to be a symbol of Judaism.

The people led by Moses did reach Canaan and founded a nation there. Around 1000 B.C.E., King David established Jerusalem as its capital city. His son, King Solomon, built the Israelites' first Great Temple in Jerusalem. The magnificent temple was constructed of stone and special woods, such as fragrant cedar. The house of worship was surrounded and protected by a wall.

When the Babylonian Empire attacked and defeated the Jewish kingdom in 586 B.C.E., the Great Temple was

Solomon's temple, as depicted in ancient times

destroyed. Many Israelites became Babylonian slaves. It took nearly 50 years for Jews to rebuild their Great Temple. When it was finished, in the 520s B.C.E., it too was surrounded by a wall, and it stood for more than 500 years.

During this time, the Jewish kingdom and Judaism itself came under attack. Antiochus IV, who had become the ruler of the Syrian portion of the Greek Empire in 175 B.C.E., tried to force the Jews to abandon their religion. His army damaged Jerusalem's Great Temple and its sacred objects.

In 165 B.C.E. Jews led by Judah Maccabee won their fight against the Syrians. According to the Talmud, one of the sacred texts of Judaism, they restored the Temple, including its sacred lamp, meant to be a light that would burn forever. Because the invaders had left only one day's worth of sacred oil, Jews feared

Judah Maccabee encouraged the Israelites during battle.

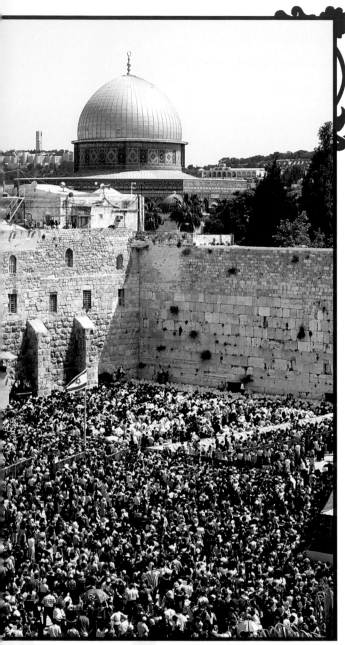

Jews often gather at Jerusalem's Western Wall to express gratitude to God or to pray for God's mercy.

the light would go out before more oil could be made pure. But because of what Jews believed was a miracle, the lamp burned brightly for eight days.

Jews today remember and celebrate this event each year with the winter festival of Hanukkah, which is also called the Festival of Lights. On eight nights, they light a special eight-branched menorah, recite prayers, eat special foods, and play games that recall Judah Maccabee's victory.

The second Great Temple remained intact until 70 C.E., when soldiers of the Roman Empire stopped a Jewish rebellion and destroyed the temple. The Western Wall— the retaining wall for the Temple mount, built in the first centuries B.C.E. and C.E. by King Herod—remained strong and vital, and so did Judaism. Today the Western Wall is a holy site for Jews around the world.

After the Roman victory, some Jews fled far from Judea and Jerusalem. Wherever they went, many tried to maintain their Jewish ways.

But important religious teachings had been lost when the Great Temple was destroyed. Rabbis wrote down these lost laws. During the next several centuries, these writings—including the rabbis' comments about them—became part of Judaism's sacred texts.

These texts don't include what Christians call the New Testament, which focuses on Jesus Christ. Many Jews respect Jesus as a historical figure, but unlike Christians, they do not believe that Jesus was the son of God. Jews still await a divine deliverer of peace and justice—the Messiah of prophecy. Jews don't believe that Jesus was the Messiah.

Chapter Three
SACRED TEXTS AND RITUALS

Judaism's most sacred text is the Torah, the first five books of the Bible, which Jews believe God gave to Moses. In English these books are called Genesis, Exodus, Leviticus, Numbers, and Deuteronomy.

The Torah tells the story of the world's creation and of God's relationship to the Jews. It includes the words of the Jewish prophets. In Hebrew Torah means law or instruction.

Traditionally the Torah is handwritten in the Hebrew language on special scrolls. In synagogues these precious scrolls are kept in a decorated cupboard called an ark. Unless it's being read or displayed during religious ceremonies, a Torah scroll is kept wrapped in a cloth. The handles of each scroll are decorated. The Torah is so highly regarded that when someone reads it, the reader's place in the text is shown by a *yad*. The tip of this long-handled metal place keeper is shaped like a tiny hand. Respectful Jews don't use their own hands to touch the words of a Torah scroll. During the Sabbath—which begins at sundown Friday and ends at sundown Saturday—and holiday services, Jews read aloud parts of the Torah and other sacred texts.

Some Jews also believe that God gave Moses the Mishnah. These rules, which explain how Jews should live, and rabbis' comments about the rules, form Judaism's second sacred text, the Talmud.

Studying the Torah and Talmud is both a

Those reading the Torah use yads to mark their places. This helps preserve the sacred text, which is often handwritten and could be smeared or damaged if touched by a person's hand.

The Shema

A short prayer from the Torah, called the *shema*, sums up the central, monotheistic belief of Judaism. The shema declares: "Hear, O Israel, the Lord is our God, the Lord is One."

Many Jews recite the shema at least twice a day in their homes. It's also part of public synagogue worship during daily services, on the Sabbath, and during holidays. The shema is also written on pieces of paper that fit into two kinds of small prayer boxes. Observant Jews place one kind, called a *mezuzah*, on the door frames of all their homes' rooms except the bathrooms and kitchens. Some Jews also wear prayer boxes called phylacteries (*tefillin* in Hebrew) on their heads and arms when they pray.

responsibility and privilege for Jews. Such study is part of the Jews' covenant with God and is not just done by rabbis or by cantors, who are experts in Jewish religious music. Because these sacred texts and study are so important in Judaism, Jews are sometimes called the People of the Book. Jews are often called the Chosen People, too, because they believe that God chose them for this covenant, and they chose to accept it.

Rabbis have various roles in Jewish communities. They study and teach the rules of behavior in the Torah and Talmud. These include laws governing diet and how food is to be prepared. Acceptable foods are labeled kosher. Many Jews don't eat pork, seafood without fins and scales, and some other meat. And many don't eat meat and milk products at the same meal.

Rabbis often lead worship services in synagogues on the weekly Sabbath, but worship service can be held without rabbis. On holidays, such as the fall's Rosh Hashana (New Year) and Yom Kippur (Day of Atonement), rabbis and cantors often lead special prayer services. In most synagogues, Jewish men wear prayer shawls and skullcaps while praying. In some synagogues, women also wear these traditional garments.

The Torah scroll, which a rabbi keeps in an ark, is the most important item in a synagogue.

Rosh Hashana and Yom Kippur

"May you have a sweet new year!" is often heard on Rosh Hashana, the Jewish New Year. Eating apples dipped in honey is another way to make this wish. During synagogue services on this important fall holiday, a ram's horn, called a *shofar*, traditionally is blown. The shofar is sounded every day except the Sabbath in the month leading up to Rosh Hashana.

The shofar also sounds 10 days later on Yom Kippur, the Day of Atonement. On this holiest day of the year, Jews ask forgiveness for their sins and resolve to do better. Observant Jews don't eat or drink on Yom Kippur. This holiday concludes what are called the Days of Awe. Jews speak about God's judging them. They wonder how they will be written about in God's Book of Life. The greeting on Yom Kippur is, "May you be inscribed for a good year!"

A rabbi blowing a shofar

Other Jewish Holidays

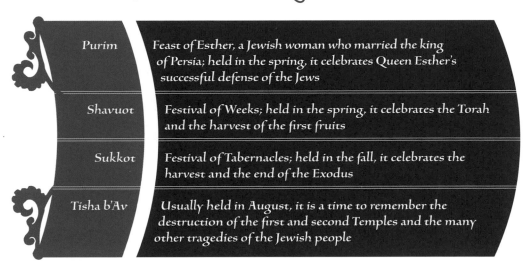

Purim	Feast of Esther, a Jewish woman who married the king of Persia; held in the spring, it celebrates Queen Esther's successful defense of the Jews
Shavuot	Festival of Weeks; held in the spring, it celebrates the Torah and the harvest of the first fruits
Sukkot	Festival of Tabernacles; held in the fall, it celebrates the harvest and the end of the Exodus
Tisha b'Av	Usually held in August, it is a time to remember the destruction of the first and second Temples and the many other tragedies of the Jewish people

Rabbis conduct the rites associated with such important events as the naming of baby girls and the circumcision of baby boys. Rabbis also preside at weddings and funerals. They help Jewish boys—and increasingly Jewish girls—prepare for their bar mitzvah or bat mitzvah ceremonies. In Hebrew bar mitzvah means "the son of the commandments," and bat mitzvah means "the daughter of the commandments." The bar mitzvah or bat mitzvah is when boys and girls officially become adult members of their religious communities. This happens automatically when boys are 13 years old and girls are 12 or 13. Bar mitzvah and bat mitzvah ceremonies are held to celebrate these events.

As adults the 12- or 13-year-olds are expected to obey the many rules set out in the Torah. They also are expected to uphold the important ideals of Judaism. These include helping the world and its people through good deeds and charity as well as through prayer and Torah study.

Boys and girls show they are ready for Jewish adulthood by studying Hebrew. They may prepare to read parts of the Torah aloud in the synagogue, or they may say a blessing over someone else's reading of the Torah

A rabbi with twins at the celebration of their bar and bat mitzvah

during a Saturday worship service. It's exciting and a bit frightening to step onto the platform in front of the Holy Ark. That's where Torah reading takes place. Family and friends are proud of these young adults. Newly bar or bat mitzvahed teens often deliver brief speeches in English. The content of these speeches varies greatly. Some young people also complete projects for charity as part of becoming bar or bat mitzvah.

After bar or bat mitzvah ceremonies, many families hold parties. These celebrations may be big or small, depending on the family and community customs.

Many important Jewish rituals take place at home. Jews greet the Sabbath with special prayers chanted over lit candles before their Friday night meal. The Passover seder is also traditionally held at home. And it's often more comfortable for families to have a baby boy's circumcision at home. Young and old alike enjoy the festivities of Hanukkah at home, watching their menorah blaze merrily.

Chapter Four
FROM DIASPORA TO RETURN

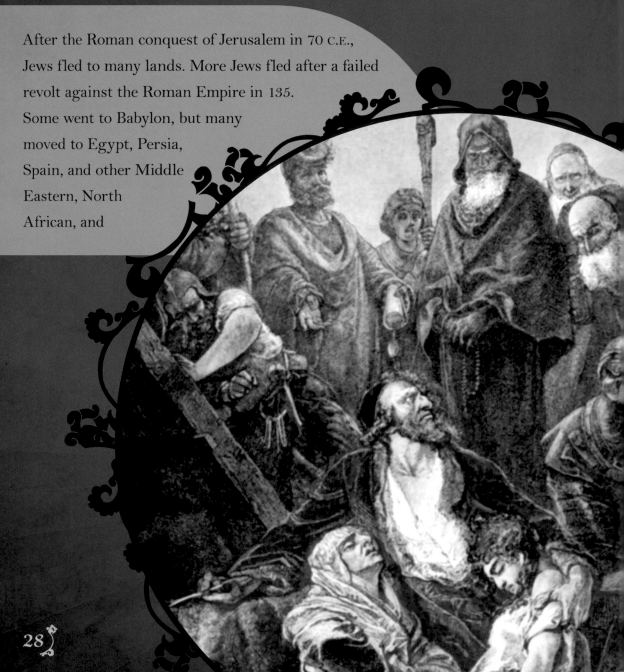

After the Roman conquest of Jerusalem in 70 C.E.,
Jews fled to many lands. More Jews fled after a failed
revolt against the Roman Empire in 135.
Some went to Babylon, but many
moved to Egypt, Persia,
Spain, and other Middle
Eastern, North
African, and

European countries. The Jews' displacement from the Holy Land and their spreading to many other countries is called the Diaspora. Even today Jews who live outside Israel are sometimes said to be part of the Diaspora.

Jews continued to move as their host countries' treatment of them changed. Between the eighth and 12th centuries, while Muslims ruled what are now Spain and Portugal, the Jewish inhabitants of those areas flourished. Jewish merchants, scholars, and doctors shared their skills and knowledge during this so-called Golden Age of Spain. They practiced their religion freely. When Christian rulers conquered this territory, though, Jews were again persecuted for their religious beliefs. Some were massacred, and others were forced to convert to Christianity. The Catholic Church in Spain established the Inquisition, a kind of religious court. Its officials hunted non-Christians and either forcibly converted them to Christianity or killed them. In 1492 Spain expelled all its Jews. Any who remained risked torture and death.

The Diaspora fostered two main traditions within Judaism. Jews living in Spain, Portugal, North Africa, and the Middle East

In 1492, the same year they sent Columbus on his famous voyage, King Ferdinand and Queen Isabella ordered that Jews, such as those depicted in this 19th century engraving, be thrown out of Spain.

Secret Jews

In Spain and Portugal, some Jews survived the Inquisition by pretending to convert to Christianity. They secretly continued to worship as Jews. These secret Jews, called crypto-Jews, were sometimes insultingly called *marranos*, which might refer to the Spanish word for pig.

came to speak Ladino, a mixture of Hebrew and Spanish. They and their descendants are known as Sephardic Jews, from the Hebrew word for Spain. Jews who lived in France, Germany, and Eastern Europe came to speak Yiddish, a mixture of Hebrew and German. They and their descendants are called Ashkenazic Jews, from the Hebrew word for Germany.

At most times and in most communities, Ashkenazic Jews were accepted by their host societies. But sometimes they suffered religious persecution and discrimination. Often they were forbidden to own land or have jobs other than money-lending. Sometimes they could live only in certain places, such as ghettos in cities or small villages in the countryside. Violent attacks on Jewish communities, called pogroms in Eastern Europe, sometimes occurred. False ideas about Jews and their practices fueled much of this hate-filled violence. Even if they were not physically attacked, Jews sometimes faced scorn when they went outside their communities. Often laws required Jews to wear special clothing or symbols, which made them easy targets for anti-Semitic (anti-Jewish) jeers and threats.

Although most Jews in the United States are Ashkenazic, the first Jews to settle in the New World were Sephardic. In 1654 a community of 23 Jews settled in the Dutch colony of New Amsterdam, later renamed New York. Their religious congregation, named Shearith Israel (Hebrew for "remnant of Israel"), is still active. Sephardic Jews have played a significant part in U.S. history since those early colonial days.

As Ashkenazic Jews sought religious and political freedom in the United States, they contributed to the country's growth. One large wave of German Jews immigrated in the 1840s and 1850s. Many Russian Jewish immigrants came to the United States in the 1880s and early 1900s, after massive pogroms in Russia. Some of these immigrants were Hasidic Jews, followers of Baal Shem Tov. At a time when some educated Jews were abandoning their Jewish identity, this 18th century

In the 1800s, many Jews left their homes in Europe to start new lives in America.

Polish rabbi had sought to bring Jews together. He counseled them to live apart from the non-Jewish world. He urged them to strengthen their personal, emotional ties to Judaism through religious song and dance.

The largest attack against Jews occurred in the 20th century. Six million Jews died in the Holocaust, a systematic mass killing that was carried out by Nazi forces led by Germany's Adolf Hitler. The death toll rose during the final years of World War II (1939 to 1945) as Hitler put into effect what he described as the "Final Solution" to the "Jewish problem." This involved moving Jews to death camps called concentration camps. There they were killed with factorylike efficiency. Murderous anti-Semitic attacks and policies, though, were frequent in Germany even before the war. They flared as soon as Hitler was elected Germany's leader in 1933. Along with Jewish lives, the Nazis destroyed synagogues, Torah scrolls, and other religious objects.

After World War II and the Holocaust, the movement to create an official Jewish nation grew stronger. In 1948 the United Nations recognized Israel as an independent country. Many European Jews who had survived the Holocaust immigrated to Israel. They

Star of David

During the Holocaust, the Nazis forced Jews to sew the six-pointed Star of David (usually in yellow) onto their clothes. This emblem made it easier for the Nazis to round up and imprison Jews. Today Jews around the world often wear the Star of David proudly as a sign of Jewish faith and identity.

Keeping the Faith During the Holocaust

Judaism flourished even in World War II concentration camps. For instance, to celebrate Hanukkah, some starving Jewish prisoners shaped menorahs out of their last potatoes and carrots. They tore strips of cloth from their ragged uniforms to use as holiday candles. As these makeshift menorahs blazed, they lightened many Jewish hearts. Prisoners remembered how—with God's help—their ancestors and religion had survived in the past. For some their wartime worship strengthened their faith and gave them hope. Some others, however, abandoned religious practice as a result of their experiences during the war.

A synagogue burned in Germany in November 1938.

joined the Jews who had settled there since the start of
the Zionist movement in the 1890s. Israel's official policy since its creation has been to welcome the return of
all Jews and to offer them citizenship. Its airlift rescues
of Ethiopian Jews during operations Moses, Joshua, and
Solomon were in line with this policy. Between 1989
and 2000, Israel welcomed nearly 1 million Jews from
the former Soviet Union. The new Israelis now make up
about 15 percent of Israel's population.

*Israeli Prime Minister David Ben-Gurion read his country's Declaration of
Independence May 14, 1948, at a Tel Aviv museum.*

Chapter Five
JUDAISM TODAY

Today most U.S. synagogues have ties with one of four denominations of organized Judaism: Orthodox, Reform, Conservative, and Reconstructionist. Orthodox Jews believe each word of the Torah is God-given.

About half of Orthodox Jews wear modern clothing and are active in all aspects of society. Some Orthodox Jews are Hasidic. They separate themselves from society and often wear garments that were typical in 18th century Poland. In all Orthodox synagogues, men and women sit apart from one another. Following ancient tradition, rabbis and cantors are male.

Reform Judaism began in early 19th century Europe. German Jews brought this branch of Judaism to the United States in the 1840s and 1850s. Reform Jews believe that the Torah was written not by God, but by faithful human beings. In Reform synagogues, men and women sit together. Since 1972, when Rabbi Sally Priesand became the first woman ordained by Reform officials, some Reform synagogues have had female rabbis as well as female cantors.

Conservative Judaism began as a middle ground between the Orthodox and Reform movements. It began in Germany in the 1850s, but it grew in the United States during the 1880s. In most Conservative synagogues, women and men sit together to worship. The Conservative movement—following the change made by Reform Judaism—ordained its first female rabbi in 1985.

Rabbi Sally Priesand was the first of nearly 1,000 women to become Reform or Conservative rabbis.

Jews gathered to pray in a synagogue.

Reconstructionist Judaism began in the United States as a 20th century offshoot of the Conservative movement. Individual rabbis and congregations often determine which customs to uphold. Women and men worship together, and women as well as men may become Reconstructionist rabbis.

Many U.S. Jews follow events in Israel with great interest. Israel today continues to face challenges. The Palestinian dispute started early in the 20th century, but it expanded with the 1948 statehood of Israel. Jewish claims to parts of the Promised Land have displaced many Palestinians from their homes. Israel's victory in 1967's Six-Day War—which led it to take over the Gaza Strip, East Jerusalem, and the West Bank of the Jordan River—deepened this conflict. Today Israelis continue

An Israeli soldier watched Palestinian refugees cross the Allenby Bridge to reach the east bank of the Jordan River in 1967. During the Six-Day War, Israel suffered about 700 deaths, while estimates of the number of Arabs killed ranged from 11,000 to 21,000, with Egyptians paying the heaviest toll.

to be attacked by some Palestinian groups, and the Israelis strike back.

This conflict is part of a larger ongoing dispute that Israel has with most of its Arabic neighboring countries. While many Arab countries recognize Israel's right to exist, they support the Palestinians. The threat of war is constant, and bloodshed occurs along Israel's borders.

Israel also struggles because of its Law of Return, which welcomes all Jews who immigrate to Israel. Conflicts sometimes occur when Jews with various backgrounds live alongside one another. Some Israelis also question the influence of Orthodox Judaism on Israel's laws. These Israelis would like to break with some Orthodox traditions, and they object when Orthodox political parties seek to expand the reach of Jewish law.

In the United States, many Jewish citizens continue to play

an active part in all walks of life. Many Jews supported
the civil rights movement of the 1950s and 1960s in this
country, and many Jews today continue to display their
concern for national and global issues.

Some Jewish leaders worry that marriage between
Jews and non-Jews has shrunk the number of Jews in

Israelis inspected damage to a classroom in the southern Israeli city
of Beersheva after a rocket attack in December 2008.

In 1993 Ruth Bader Ginsburg became the second woman to serve on the U.S. Supreme Court and the first Jewish justice since 1969.

the United States and elsewhere. The children of such marriages may choose not to continue Jewish traditions. Others argue that intermarriage has resulted in conversions, actually increasing the Jewish population. In any case, the influence of Judaism and its values has always been vast—far exceeding the religion's small percentage of the world's population. The ideals of this first monotheistic religion have influenced peoples and other religions around the globe.

The Jewish Calendar

In the fall of 2009, Jews around the world celebrate the year 5770. This is the number of years since creation, as measured by the Jewish calendar. Jews calculate this number by adding the ages of people in the Bible.

Yet even Orthodox Jews do not insist that the world is only 5,770 years old. They say we cannot know the actual length of those first seven "days" of creation described in the Torah. The Jewish calendar is used for religious purposes by Jews around the world.

TIMELINE

Circa 2000 B.C.E.	According to the Torah, Abraham moves his people from the Fertile Crescent (now mostly Israel, Jordan, Syria, and Iraq) to Canaan (now roughly Israel and Lebanon)
Circa 1000 B.C.E.	King David makes Jerusalem the capital of Judah
165 B.C.E.	Judah Maccabee fights Antiochus and Syrians
Circa 70 C.E.	Rabbis in Palestine begin to write down and add to oral laws, creating the Talmud
1492	Jews are expelled from Spain
1840s and 1850s	Large numbers of German Jews arrive in the United States, bringing Reform Judaism with them
1933	Adolf Hitler becomes chancellor of Germany; anti-Semitism is put into practice and law
1945	The Holocaust, which killed more than 6 million Jews and members of other persecuted groups, ends with Germany's defeat in World War II
1948	The state of Israel is established
1967	The Six-Day War breaks out between Israel and its Arab neighbors
1991	Operation Solomon, an airlift of Ethiopian Jews to Israel, is accomplished
2009	Rabbi Julie Schoenfeld becomes the first female vice president of the Rabbinical Assembly, the Conservative movement's organization of rabbis

Abraham's people called themselves Hebrews, which means "people from the other side." They came from the distant side of the Euphrates River in the Fertile Crescent. The Bible refers to them as the Children of Israel. The word Jew came into use centuries later. It stems from the name of Abraham's great-grandson Judah.

When Columbus set sail in 1492, the interpreter who accompanied him—Luis de Torres—was a Jew. He had been expelled from Spain that year, along with all other Jews.

Some people divide Sephardic Jews into two categories. They still call Jews from Spain and Portugal Sephardim, but they call Jews from Northern Africa and the Middle East Misrachim or Misrachic Jews.

Twelve-year-old Judith Kaplan was the first girl to publicly celebrate her bat mitzvah in the United States. She recited her Torah portion in a Manhattan synagogue in March 1922.

The first "talking" Hollywood movie shown in 1927, *The Jazz Singer*, was about a Jewish family and its entertainer son. The son is at first a cantor, an expert in Jewish religious songs.

The dates of Jewish holidays shift slightly each year because the Jewish religious calendar is based on moon cycles.

GLOSSARY

anti-Semitic—ideas or actions filled with hatred and scorn of Jews and Judaism

bar mitzvah, bat mitzvah—time when a boy or girl reaches Jewish adulthood

cantor—expert in Jewish religious songs; cantors lead parts of worship

circumcision—surgical removal of the foreskin of a penis

Conservative—one of the major movements of Judaism; followers accept the binding nature of Jewish law but believe that the law can change

covenant—formal agreement between people or between people and God

denomination—branch of a religion

Inquisition—arm of the Catholic Church organized in 15th century Spain to eliminate non-Christians

kosher—permitted food for Jews, as defined by rules in the Torah

matzoh—unleavened bread eaten during Passover to remember the Exodus from Egypt

Messiah—divine deliverer of peace and justice; Christians believe that Jesus was the Messiah

Mishnah—oral Torah that Jews believe God handed down to them

Orthodox—one of the major movements of Judaism; followers believe that Jewish law comes from God and cannot be changed

patriachs—founding fathers of a religion or group of people

phylacteries—small prayer boxes worn on the forehead and arm, in accord with the Torah

pogroms—anti-Semitic attacks on groups of Eastern European Jews

Reconstructionist—one of the major movements of Judaism; followers believe Jewish law was created by people rather than by God

Reform—one of the major movements of Judaism; followers believe that Jewish law was inspired by God and one can choose which laws to follow

synagogue—Jewish house of worship

Talmud—second sacred text of Judaism, consisting of the oral Torah (Mishnah) and rabbis' commentary on these rules

Torah—Judaism's most sacred text, also referred to by non-Jews as the first five books of the Hebrew Bible or the Old Testament

Zionist—19th and 20th century movement for a Jewish homeland in Palestine; it helped to create modern Israel

FURTHER REFERENCE

Nonfiction

Barnes, Trevor. *Judaism: Worship, Festivals, and Ceremonies From Around the World.* Boston: Kingfisher, 2005.

Hoffman, Lawrence A., and Ron Wolfson. *What You Will See Inside a Synagogue.* Woodstock, Vt.: SkyLight Paths Pub. and Jewish Lights Pub., 2004.

Langley, Myrtle. *Eyewitness Religion.* New York: DK Publishing, 2005.

Fiction

Hesse, Karen. *Brooklyn Bridge.* New York: Feiwel and Friends, 2008.

Orlev, Uri. *The Man From the Ohter Side.* New York: Puffin Books, 1995.

Taylor, Sydney. *All-of-a-Kind-Family.* New York: Delacorte Press, 2005.

Internet Sites

FactHound offers a safe, fun way to find Internet sites related to this book. All of the sites on FactHound have been researched by our staff.

Here's all you do:

Visit *www.facthound.com*

FactHound will fetch the best sites for you!

ABOUT THE AUTHOR

Natalie M. Rosinsky is the award-winning author of more than 100 publications. These include *Hinduism*, books about 10 Native American tribes, *Write Your Own Myth*, and *Write Your Own Fable*. She lives and works in Mankato, Minnesota. Natalie earned graduate degrees from the University of Wisconsin-Madison and has been a high school teacher and college professor as well as a corporate trainer.